The Watchful Heart

'Modern Spirituality' series

The Watchful Heart

DAILY READINGS WITH RUTH BURROWS

Introduced and edited by
Elizabeth Ruth Obbard

Darton, Longman and Todd
London

First published in 1988 by
Darton, Longman and Todd Ltd
89 Lillie Road, London SW6 1UD

© 1988 Ruth Burrows

Introduction and arrangement
© 1988 Elizabeth Ruth Obbard

ISBN 0 232 51773 8

British Library Cataloguing in Publication Data

Burrows, Ruth
    The watchful heart.
    1. Christian life—Daily readings
    I. Title   II. Series   III. Obbard,
    Elizabeth Ruth
    242'.2

    ISBN 0-232-51773-8

Phototypeset by Input Typesetting Ltd
London SW19 8DR
Printed and bound in Great Britain by
Anchor Brendon Ltd, Tiptree, Essex

Contents

Introduction

I had spent twelve years in religious life, when a copy of Ruth Burrows's first book came into my hands. I can still remember as vividly as if it were yesterday, sitting on the bed in my room, turning the pages in bewilderment and wonder as I read, and thinking to myself: Here is someone with courage who tells the real truth. Here was depicted a woman whose situation had been far from ideal, who would seem to have been handicapped by a cramping religious system and a super-sensitive temperament, yet who had faced up to life in all its reality and in and through it found God in such a way that she could assert: 'One long, searching look into my past and I see, there in its depths, the face of Christ gazing back at me.'

This was my first introduction to the inner growth of the woman who would be my Novice-Mistress in Carmel: the Carmel in which I had found myself almost by accident and which had struck me immediately by its breadth of spirit, its human warmth and its atmosphere of trust and acceptance.

So through many of my formative years I had the opportunity not only to live with Ruth Burrows but to share her insights and, later, her friendship. But that first impression of her absolute dedication to the truth has never left me; rather, it has deepened over the years, and I find in all her writings that intensely personal approach, born of contemplative life lived within a community and within a distinctive spiritual tradition. She is humble, for her whole approach is rooted in the reality of the human condition of vulnerability and need. I can think of no better summary of her teaching than what she herself says in the Introduction to her first book:

> ... What I want to show people is that what really matters is trust in God; that this trust cannot be there until we have lost all self-trust and are rooted in poverty; that we must be willing to go to God with empty hands, and that the whole meaning of our existence and the one consuming desire of the heart of God is that *we should let ourselves be loved* [italics mine].

In *Before the Living God* Ruth Burrows draws out the personal implications of this passage in her own life and I can think of no better way to know her own journey than to read the complete book with its honest evaluation of a path travelled by a vulnerable and searching woman.

From that first autobiography, which is more in the nature of a spiritual *Aeneid*, Ruth Burrows has gone on to become one of today's foremost religious writers and an exponent of the purest Carmelite tradition.

A phenomenon of recent years has been the increased interest in prayer and meditation. There has been a turning towards the East in search of techniques which enable modern men and women to relax and 'enter into the Divine Mind'. In contrast Ruth Burrows shows clearly that there is already in Western Christianity a largely neglected corpus of mystical writers who eschew 'techniques' and point out the authentic Christian approach to union with God. Among such writers of unparalleled authority are Teresa of Avila and John of the Cross. They are recognized as classic teachers of Christian prayer, but their language and forms of expression are 'dated' and so their work is often unintelligible to those who need a sure guide but live and think in a different cultural framework. It is in this area that Ruth Burrows's main contribution to modern spiritual literature lies.

As a Carmelite herself, she is thoroughly imbued with the works of Teresa and John, and their nineteenth-century counterpart, Thérèse of Lisieux. Her own life, spent in Carmel since her late teens, has witnessed her struggle to equate the kernel of these mystical writers with pure gospel teaching, placing them too in the context of modern psychological insights. In her expositions on prayer she has been able to take mysticism clearly out of the esoteric world of psychic experience and place it firmly in real life and the Scriptures.

Two of her major works, *Interior Castle Explored* and *Ascent to Love*, are contemporary interpretations of Teresa of Avila's *Interior Castle* and John of the Cross's *Ascent of Mount Carmel*. In these she examines the classic teaching on prayer of these two masters of spirituality and shows how they can guide us today as surely as they guided their sixteenth-century contemporaries. As Carmel is an Order dedicated to continual prayer, so it is only to be expected that it should produce men and women who are willing to give God everything – but this is not something reserved for professional pray-ers, it is the destiny of all who live a serious Christian life. Ruth Burrows will admit of no 'second-class citizens' in the path to union with God!

Guidelines to Mystical Prayer which followed on her first book was written in conjunction with 'Claire and Petra', two obvious pseudonyms for two different types of person whom Ruth Burrows classifies under the original terms 'Light-on and Light-off' to designate those mystics who 'see' God in a non-conceptual manner and those whose path lies through the way of darkness or 'non-seeing'. Using these terms she then explores the so-called 'mystical experiences' and shows how these in themselves have merely a psychic base and are no criterion for assessing closeness to God. Another original metaphor in this book is the division of the classic three stages of the mystical life into three islands, each completely separate except for a bridge between the first and the second. Here again the book is largely biographical in nature, hence its perennial appeal, for we see the life of prayer as worked out in practice, not merely in theory!

To Believe in Jesus is a basic text for introducing a person to the beginnings of the Christian life – which is true to tradition in that it holds up the ideal of union with God as the heritage of *all* and shows how to approach the whole question of faith in a mature and adult manner.

Two further books, *Living Love* and *Our*

Father, are mainly collections of conferences to her community, but as she says, since all are called to a life of prayer and total self-giving, they too are applicable to people who live what are often termed 'ordinary lives'.

As with all writers, there are some themes which predominate even while she expresses the classic Carmelite teaching on prayer, especially as enunciated by John of the Cross and Teresa of Avila. One is the theme beloved by the latter which cannot be obscured even by her flights of effusive rhetoric: that is, the centrality of Jesus, and that growth in prayer is growth in knowledge of and friendship with him. Here Ruth Burrows is adamant that techniques of prayer are irrelevant, as is any method which wishes to contact the Divine and bypass the human Jesus who alone is the Way, the Truth and the Life. In fact, to seek any 'experience' or special revelation of God for oneself is useless, for God has already revealed all he has to reveal in his Son (cf. John of the Cross). There is no more to be had in the way of favours and revelations. Therefore, to cling to Jesus is the heart of Christian life and prayer. There is no short-cut. Hence Ruth Burrows emphasizes such things as study of the Scriptures (all too easily overlooked in a certain fundamentalist or charismatic approach to God) and openness to the Word in life and liturgy. The sacraments are indispensable for they are objective rather than subjective. Christ is among us today just as he was 2000 years ago, if only we exercise our faith.

Practical love of neighbour and an emphasis on community might seem surprising in a Carmelite, but contemplative life is essentially lived in community and closely bound up with others at all levels. Here again Ruth Burrows is only putting the teaching of John and Teresa in modern idiom and linking it with the Gospels. Any way of prayer which would bypass other people cannot possibly be authentic.

A word which comes up continually in all her writing is *faith* and its more usual counterpart, *trust*. Reading through all she has written, I think these words – faith and trust – would be those which predominate. The modern world is a technological one, at least in the West. Many areas of life which in the past seemed to be under God's direct control are now in the hands of human beings. Here is a chance for growth in pure faith, since a certain 'magical' element in religion can no longer be upheld. Faith is worked out in daily life by a growing trust in God. We trust him by handing our lives over completely to him, asking for no 'proofs', allowing him to control our lives more and more. On the human level this is experienced as great poverty of spirit, a self-knowledge based on truth which does not puff us up and exalt the ego but allows God to come to us in all our neediness. To trust God in our nakedness and shame is to open ourselves to his inpouring love which is only kept at bay by barricades of our own devising. Trust is the one thing which allows us to accept ourselves as we are and God as he is.

Another of Ruth Burrows's themes is that of fidelity to prayer for God's sake rather than for any benefit which might accrue to self. For her, this fidelity in darkness is proof of a love which seeks nothing but the Beloved, and she is eager to have her readers give time faithfully to prayer come what may. Life and prayer cannot be separated; they are intermingled and flow into each other and each tests the other for authenticity.

Of course, none of these themes are new, but Ruth Burrows treats of them so that they hit home in a unique way. Her books have been the means of introducing the spiritual classics and the kernel of the mystical doctrine of the Carmelite writers to an audience which would otherwise find them irrelevant or incomprehensible. There are also her original insights into the nature of the mystical experience and its scriptural basis which is essential for correct interpretation.

However, I would wish to add to this on a personal level. Ruth Burrows finds Christ in her own experience of life 'as it is'. Therefore our aim must be not merely to see how he has worked in *her* life and insights but in our own. In other words we have to trust *our own* experience of God and life, and this in practice may be quite different on the emotional level from hers – so much depends on individual temperament and giftedness.

Each individual growth is unique, and it *is* a growth rather than a breaking/remaking image that is used. Hence Ruth Burrows can say truthfully that many people can come to deep union with God by way of a well-nigh imperceptible development. It is the gospel image of the seed in the earth, the leaven in the yeast, the harvest of wheat and tares. To root out the tares prematurely by a harsh, self-denying régime (which is often taken for fervour in religious matters) can stunt a person's whole development. In this area, her interpretation of John of the Cross and the way of nothingness is revealing. We often try to snap tensions that should remain and be worked through, but we can be tempted to avoid the pain of risk and failure by too rigorous a self-denial. God does not want us to bypass the normal means of human growth: friendship, love, work, responsibility, joy, affirmation, sorrow . . . in favour of some pseudo way of renunciation which stunts us as persons and deprives us of the capacity to respond to each situation as it arises. We *cannot* know all the answers in advance, much as we might like to!

Some of Ruth Burrows's best work, in my opinion, lies in her day-to-day application of the Gospel to Carmelite life, which is basically the ordinary daily round lived in an environment which maintains a fine balance between solitude and community and which is a microcosm of the Christian life as a whole. In this area she reveals too a deep identification with Mary, image of the contemplative, the perfect disciple. Occasionally it may seem that her writings carry a depth of seriousness which excludes joy, but this is not so in reality. A careful reading shows that she points the way to living in the world of faith where *all* is joy, because Jesus is risen and with his Father.

In conclusion, when choosing these short passages I have tried to concentrate on those extracts from her writings which will provide food for daily thought and prayer. Therefore I have not touched on her theories of 'Light-on, Light-off', nor on the image of the three islands. These are best read in full context, and though they are integral to her own teaching they did not seem to have a place in a book such as this. What I have chosen gives, I think, the best of her insights into the life of faith and her application of traditional Carmelite spirituality to the life of modern men and women seeking God in prayer.

'Consider, and it is true, that God gives himself to those who give up everything for him,' wrote St Teresa over 400 years ago. Then she adds the telling sentence which Ruth Burrows would certainly echo: 'God is not an accepter of persons; he loves all; there is no excuse for anyone.' For those who wish to love God, there must be fostered the deep conviction that he has loved them first and only awaits their response to the intimacy he so desires to lead them to.

ELIZABETH RUTH OBBARD
Carmel of Our Lady of Walsingham
Norfolk

One in Christ

We human beings are not isolated individuals in God's sight; we are his dear family, of whom Jesus is the first-born and head.

Love is our supreme and only law, the love which Jesus revealed, and our destiny lies in intimate fellowship with the Father even in this life, expanding into perfect fulfilment when 'the Kingdom of God comes'.

Those of the family, privileged to know its blessedness, who bear the name of Christ, rejoicing in the re-creation he brings, are sent out to be the Light of the World. They know, each of them, that they are called to the fullness of love and holiness following the poor, humble, cross-bearing Jesus.

Living in the world they must bear responsibility for it, working for the welfare of others in whatever way they can.

Their faith in the Risen One enables them to combat evil confidently wherever it is met, for contrary to all appearances the victory of the Risen Lord dominates the world.

Each task well done, each talent developed, each advance in the mastery of the world's energies, each effort to improve the human condition, all are contributing to God's great design: the resurrection and transformation of the human race.

Taking God seriously

Faith is not a thing of the mind, it is not an intellectual certainty or a felt conviction of the heart. It is a sustained decision to take God with utter seriousness as the God of our life; it is to live out the hours in a practical, concrete affirmation that he is Father and he is 'in heaven'.

It is a decision to shift the centre of our life from ourselves to him, to forgo self-interest and make his interest, his will our sole concern. This is what it means to hallow his name as Father in heaven.

Often it may seem that we only act 'as if', so unaffected are our hearts, perhaps even mocking us: 'Where is your God?' It is this acting 'as if' which is true faith.

All that matters to faith is that God should have what he wants and we know that what he wants is always our own blessedness.

His purposes are worked out, his will mediated to us in the humblest form, as humble as our daily bread.

Responding in faith

What God reveals is for living and only for living, not to adorn books or cultivate the human mind. What God reveals is himself, as a lover reveals himself to the beloved.

God summons us to a love relationship and this summons of love demands a response of our whole person in the whole of our living. Human life has no other meaning than to be a response to the God who calls us to love.

Faith covers every aspect of our relation to God in our earthly existence: from its beginning, which is the grace to accept Jesus of Nazareth as God's messenger, to that encounter with him which must surely come if we are faithful, an encounter which means a going down with him into death, in order to rise with him in perfect fulfilment when, still in this world, 'I lay hold of that for which Christ laid hold of me'.

If the essence of the divine goal is an embrace of love, faith is the arms with which we enfold the beloved.

Wanting the truth

How do we attain to intimacy with God, or rather, how do we enter into the intimacy offered?

We must be certain that no wooing is necessary. We do not have to find ways of attracting the divine partner, of getting him to notice us. Here is someone who is love itself and the very fount of our existence, enfolding us, inviting us to receive him, drawing us to his heart.

Scripture and mystical writers have used the different modes of love and friendship — parent/child, husband/wife, brother, friend — to tell us something of the reality of God's love and desire for us. Each is inadequate. All together they are inadequate.

It is not easy to speak properly of a deep human relationship; how much more so when one of the partners is God! And even if one were able, through profound experience and intensive thought and effort, to give what seems as close approximation to the truth as possible, its understanding depends on the heart of the recipient.

Truth must find an echo in the one who hears it if it is to be recognized. Put it another way: a heart must be really listening, really wanting the truth, really wanting God.

Approaching prayer

Most of us find it almost impossible not to think of prayer as a special activity of life, an art that can be taught or learned rather as we can learn to play a musical instrument. So some of us are quick to feel we are proficient and others that we are painfully handicapped, are missing out on some secret or have some lack in our nature which makes prayer difficult if not impossible for us.

We feel there are certain laws governing prayer, techniques to be mastered, and when we have got hold of these we can pray. Thus we look around for the guru, for the one who has mastered the art and its techniques, and eagerly wait to be taught.

When we take up a book or article on prayer we shall probably detect, if we stop to think, that we are looking for the key, the magic formula that is going to put our prayer right, enable us to 'make a go' of this mysterious activity called prayer.

All this is proof that we are overlooking the fundamental fact that prayer is not a technique but a relationship; that there is no handicap, no obstacle, no problem. The only problem is that we do not want God. We may want a 'spiritual life', we may want 'prayer', but we do not want God.

All anyone can do for us, any guru teach us, is to keep our eyes on Jesus, God's perfect, absolute friend.

The mystery of inner poverty

We imagine a life of prayer to be a growing enrich-
ment — increased light on divine things, on God;
whereas in reality prayer is experienced as a
growing impoverishment. In this state we must be
gentle and tolerant, simply offering ourselves to
God as we are, sure of his tender love.

We are content to remain always poor if he so
wishes, certain that he will stoop down and indeed
is stooping down to fill us with himself. The Spirit
pleads for us with 'sighs beyond all words'.

God asks of us but a silent, lone watching of the
heart day after day, in sunshine and in rain. He
wants to find us always there, a faithful, loving
presence.

We can think of the world as a sick child and
ourselves as the tireless mother at its bedside. It
wakes and finds her there, wakes again, she is still
there. God communicates to us his own motherhood, his patient, self-giving love. We all know
that such a love is worth more than ecstatic
raptures.

God wants us to tend, nurture, purify the world,
but for that our own hearts must first be tempered
and set on fire. Let us allow him to work in us
without bitterness or resentment on our part.
Mary will help us. No one understands as she the
mystery of love which is given to those who are
poor and needy.

To be as Mary is

Mary of Nazareth – a nobody – is shown as being addressed by God, invited; the word fructifies in her. Her natural motherhood is a sacrament or symbol of the deeper reality of spiritual maternity. Luke uses her as John uses the figure of the beloved disciple. When we see her in Luke's Gospel and as countless paintings depict her, addressed by the angel, bowing her head in submission, bringing forth Jesus, bearing him in her arms, nourishing him, we are meant to say 'That is I'.

Do we dare? Our Lady of Vladimir, for instance: a picture of intimacy – the divine child pressed against her cheek, whispering his secrets, and her grave eyes, reflecting something of the weight of those secrets, turned out upon the world. If we really believe Jesus' words we must say that Mary stands for me, what God wants to give me, to do with me. There is absolutely no difference in any way that really matters.

I no longer call you servants, but friends, because everything I have learned from my Father I communicate to you.

Mother, sister, brother, spouse – all these relationships of closeness: we need them all and more to get even an iota of the idea of the intimacy offered to us. To be truly, fully Christian is to be all that at once. We have the capacity to be as Mary is!

Heart of a mother

The deepest element in woman is self-giving, other-centredness, and it is towards this we must ever tend with Mary's help and example.

To give some idea of motherhood's self-sacrifice in which we must excel I quote a translation from a French poem which is quaint but very profound.

'A son has torn the heart out of his mother's breast because his loved one wanted it. Turning away he stumbles and drops the heart and the mother's heart anxiously asks, "Did you hurt yourself, my child?" '

That might prove a very profitable meditation on the fount of all maternal love – God himself.

I use this poem as a little example to help us realize the abyss of self-sacrifice motherhood demands. Mother-love asks nothing for self. It finds its reward in being allowed to love, to give, to die.

Becoming Jesus

Each of us has to become Jesus. This is the Christian's sole aim which is nothing other than the destiny of all people; it is what human beings are for, what the world is for. This is the essence of all effective apostolate — to live the depth and breadth of the human vocation.

When we say 'Jesus' we are holding together two profound realities. We mean the living Lord in the glory of his victory, the surrendered One who is all God's. Our roots are in this victorious One. He is the ground on which we stand, the unshakable rock, our perfect security.

But the Risen Jesus is lost to our human gaze. He is in light inaccessible which our poor earthly sight cannot cope with. And we are not meant to try.

Standing on his victory, drawing our life from his inexhaustible well-spring, we are gently turned away from him in his splendour to contemplate him in his earthly existence.

This is what we do when we meditate on the Gospels. This is how we meet him, learn from him. We learn from him in the days of his flesh when he too must contemplate the mystery of the Father, not face to face but in a mirror darkly as we do.

Jesus, revelation of the Father

In former times God used various ways to enlighten us, but now he has spoken once for all by his Son. All other modes of communication are abolished. Formerly God could not make himself understood; there was no one of sufficient transparency to receive him. Now there is. Jesus is the definitive revelation of God; God has nothing more to reveal.

You crave to know, be reassured, have a guarantee? Jesus will satisfy it. You look within at your own subjective feelings, but what do they tell you? They can give no certitude. You have all the guarantee you need in Jesus.

See what he has shown us of the Father's steadfast love, of his will to give us everything. See how he reveals the Father as total forgiveness. What need have you of further reassurance? You seek to know how to please God in all you do – then look to Jesus.

There is scarcely anyone who does not depart from the way of pure faith and seek some subjective revelation or assurance. There is no greater security, consolation or happiness than to lean absolutely on Jesus the Man.

Living knowledge

Until the very last stage of all, the state of spiritual marriage, there is always a danger of bypassing Jesus. We can still find the rawly human a scandal and the crucified Christ anathema, even though we hail him with our minds and lips.

In the last stage this is impossible. The perfect are one with Jesus, inseparable from him; he *is* them – their Way, their Truth, their Life. A living knowledge of Jesus is the very heart of union.

This knowledge is mystical, infused, but the loving heart goes on seeking to know more, chiefly through Scripture.

'There are depths in Christ to be fathomed. He is an inexhaustible mine with many recesses full of treasures, and however deeply we descend we shall never reach the end' (John of the Cross).

Such knowledge as this is living, springing as it does from a sharing in his self-emptying.

A *new vision*

To commit ourselves to Jesus and the Father whom he reveals means a deliberate choosing to move off ourselves, to refuse to stand on ourselves, to be our own judges of reality.

We have to discover Jesus' vision and make it our own even against what our senses and reason tell us. It means trying to live our human lives as he lived his in obedience to the Father.

Faith has no reality if it is not love. Love chooses. Love moves out of self to the other; it is a movement of surrender.

Faith, hope and love: these are different aspects of the one human surrender to the God of love.

Biblical faith is not a mere intellectual assent to this or that piece of information; it is an act of the whole person surrendering to the God who calls in love, or rather, offers himself in love. It is the human 'yes' to the infinite mystery of love. It is obedience.

'Yes' in the Lord

Jesus, holy and beloved,
Hold me always in your 'yes'.
Let nothing matter to me from this moment
But the Father's good pleasure,
The coming of his Kingdom.
Let me not matter to myself.
I have only one short life in which to love
In difficulty and pain,
Trusting in the dark and non-seeming.
Opportunities come and pass forever,
Never to return.
Let me not miss one,
Let my life be lived in total love.

There is no other way of living a truly human life.

All is God's work

If we look at what John of the Cross has to say about the transformed soul, one on the summit of the mountain, this is what we get. The Bride has no desires of the will, no acts of understanding, neither object nor occupation of any kind which she does not refer wholly to God, together with all her desires.

She is absorbed in God, all love. All her actions are love, all her energies and strength are intent on love. She has given up everything for the pearl of great price, total union with God.

She is never seeking her own gratification, her will is wanting his will alone. 'My sole occupation is love', 'I do always the things that please him'.

When we think of such selflessness, such love for God, we must, naturally speaking, feel only despair. It is impossible to achieve. But God wants it in us and everything is possible to God.

Here we touch the heart of Christianity and mysticism. It is all God's work. He wills it absolutely and we must choose to let him do it.

Contemplation and faith

All too easily when we talk about the interior life of prayer or contemplation we have in mind some sort of refined human activity going on within; it can be cultivated and grow to wonderful proportions.

But let us substitute the words 'interior life' for 'depth life' and we come nearer to what it means to be a contemplative. A contemplative lives below the surface, is present to what really is and not in the ephemeral, often illusory world of impressions.

Contemplation is based on faith. Only faith takes us behind appearances; only faith roots us in naked reality and keeps us there steadfastly, refusing to allow us to escape into pleasant fantasy, to make excursions into 'if only', into what our ego wants for its satisfaction and comfort.

Faith says: You are for God. You must abandon all desire to cling to boundaries, to your own limits, your own idea of things. You have to allow yourself all the time to be drawn up and away, or down and beyond, to God himself.

Signs of the Spirit

Our innate desire is to have something for ourselves, of ourselves. Often enough what lies behind 'favours' and a preoccupation with them is a deep desire for assurance. We feel these things authenticate our spiritual life. They do not. Nothing we experience in the spiritual life is itself any guarantee.

We have no guarantee except God's love and fidelity. He does not want us to have any but this. We turn from him when we make much of such things, when we crave them and welcome them. Too easily they induce spiritual pride simply because we read in them signs of great spirituality. We must be convinced they are no such sign.

The true signs of the Spirit are very different: an ever-growing selflessness in daily living, self-disregard in all spheres, humility, service, devotedness, and in our inmost heart a joy at being empty of all, poor, abandoned to God as he appears at every moment and in whatever guise.

The desert path

St John of the Cross tells us that the desert is an excellent training ground, a teacher of discipline. The Book of Exodus illustrates this point.

The desert offers little satisfaction to the senses: there we learn quickly that God alone suffices and so we attain true wisdom. In silence, solitude and detachment we experience our weakness. We are without support, hungry and desolate.

Like Hagar we can cry aloud to God and like Elijah cast ourselves down exhausted and discouraged; but we also become aware of a Presence which fills the desert, ever watchful, ever tender.

So does God answer our childlike cry and show us to a fountain of living water at which to quench our thirst; so does he feed us with living bread to strengthen and comfort us on our lonely journey.

God provides

We must submit our whole being to the discipline
of the desert and not seek to avoid it. Like the
Israelites of old we must press forward along a
way we know not, trusting ourselves to God's
guidance, relying on him to supply all our needs.

Alas! Like them we can grow weary of the wilderness, but let us not lose hope. Let us leave it to
God to give us sufficient pleasure and comfort to
sustain us. He will send us manna and make sweet
water spring from the rock in due time, when we
really need it.

We learn by experience that there is beauty and
tenderness even in the desert, but it must be of
God's providing. Let us accept with humble love
all the comforts both material and spiritual which
he provides for us but let us not seek them for
ourselves.

Oftentimes the silence and bleakness of the desert
seems to penetrate into the depths of our souls, a
desert of loneliness and aridity. We must not try
to evade this suffering; just trust in God to see us
through, putting a seal upon our lips, letting the
silent peace of the desert enfold us.

Only Jesus

On the Mount of the Transfiguration the disciples 'looking up, saw no one but only Jesus'. The desert prepares us for such an encounter.

Jesus calls us to be with him continually in his lonely hours of prayer on the mountain. Others he sends away to the comfort of their homes, but not us. We have no earthly home. He alone is home for us. With Jesus we climb the mountain of prayer at dawn, at midday, at night, in rain and sunshine, in weariness and joy.

This is a myrrh-scented mountain, an incense-breathing hill, for the fragrance of sacrifice is mingled with adoring prayer. Often Jesus only asks that we keep him company, identifying ourselves with his adoration, his love, his intercession for all.

Whatever we may feel we know it is always good for us, our glory and our joy, to be with him, the supreme Adorer.

The beauty of Carmel

Carmel is a garden — not a bleak and arid waste-land but a wilderness abounding in verdure, fruit and flowers.

The bleakness is but apparent. The more we surrender to the law of the desert, the more we strive after detachment from all things, the more faithful we are to prayer, the more we shall delight in the beauty of Carmel.

The spirit of Carmel is not harsh, it is sweet, 'sweeter than honey'. Our Lady is the most beautiful flower of Carmel but each of us too is a flower in this garden with a beauty and fragrance peculiarly her own.

Carmel is a garden in the wilderness for God alone. All that grows there is his alone. Let us never want to be seen, known, admired, for we belong only to him. 'Count me no more than a wild rose on the lowland plain, a wild lily on the mountain slopes.' This is our sole joy.

Let us never underestimate the great gift of God in calling us to this garden land where our whole lives can be surrendered to him in solitude, prayer and virginal fruitfulness for the whole Church.

Continual intercession

If a nun withdraws from the world's activities it is only that she may live more intensely at its heart; and the joys and hopes, the griefs and anxieties of the men and women of the age are hers.

By the gift of herself to Christ and his growing dominion over her, her sensibilities are refined, and her womanly qualities of compassion, concern for others and self-sacrificing love are immeasurably increased.

Uprooted, free, she must, with Mary the Mother of the Lord and his most perfect disciple, ponder in her heart God's revelation so that the torch of true wisdom, which is the insight of love, may burn brightly on the earth.

Her vocation is to intercede for mankind not merely by word but by her very being.

Striving to live surrendered and exposed to God she is purified by him, and in profound impoverishment learns experimentally that 'none is good but God alone' and 'without me you can do nothing'.

Entering into mystery

We ourselves are mystery and our proper ambience is mystery. When we speak of God's hiddenness we are saying he is the answer to our yearnings. He is unfathomable mystery offered to us.

Through Jesus he reveals himself not only as our Beloved — the object of desire — but as our Lover. Then we realize that he has always been our Beloved for the simple reason that he *is* our Lover.

We learn that there is a fulfilment to our endless longings but not within ourselves, not within the limitations of this world or our own achievements, but as pure gift.

There is an inevitable conflict between our true self and its deepest desire to be enfolded, possessed by our Beloved, and the innate desire to control, to possess, to find fulfilment within ourselves, of ourselves.

This we can call the ego. It is our basic self-orientation which is a dead end. But it is precisely our nature to go *beyond* the limits of our nature so as to enter into God! The self must triumph over the ego.

Total commitment

We stand by Jesus in verbal affirmation and in liturgical ceremony, but each of us has to examine how far our actual commitment squares with what we profess.

We are committed – up to a point; we follow him – up to a point; but we have not yet cast ourselves absolutely, irrevocably, onto his side.

Think about it: those seemingly small but pernicious criticisms, those quick retorts expressive more of indignation and aggrieved pride than of pure love, the allowing of resentful thoughts and feelings, playing with mistrust, depression, discouragement, instead of a loyal rejection of such things.

God's grace is always flowing plentifully. Each morning there are special outpourings. Let us determine that today will see an end of our equivocation and the beginning of an unswerving discipleship.

Let us go to die with him.

True worship

Outward worship of itself avails nothing. We have to pay attention, apply our minds to God's service: the whole of ourselves must be brought to bear on our loving service of him. This cannot be done without great labour.

Day by day, hour by hour, we must be renewing the offering of ourselves, making sure it is not a matter of words and sentiments, but actuality. Everything we do from morning to night must be truthful, coming from our deepest centre.

How few of us, says St Thérèse, always do our best, never take little holidays, but are *always* attentive to God, present to him, waiting on him, loving him.

This is the living sacrifice, holy and acceptable, the pure spiritual worship which alone matters to him.

The reality of the sacraments

The great central act of our religion is not of our devising, it is given to us. We do not have to make our worship; we enter into, claim as our own, a worship God himself has given to us. God has done and does everything for us; all is pure grace. The sacraments affirm this.

Never are we more truly Christian than when we approach the sacraments with the Christian community. This is where God 'touches' us. Here, at this moment, is our guarantee.

What need have we of a word spoken inwardly when we hear the word spoken outwardly: 'My Body for you', 'Your sins are forgiven'.

Our religion is historical; earthly because divine. God affirms the whole of our human being, wants it all, sanctifies it all, comes to us through its reality. In our sacred liturgy we have the concrete certainty of divine encounter and action. We are grounded on objectivity rather than on the quicksands of our poor subjectivity which can, in certain states, seem so sure, so divine.

Joy in the Eucharist

The symbol of the Eucharist is life and joy. Bread satisfies, wine elates and both produce gladness of heart. The joy of each individual is intensified by the joy of the whole.

In the Eucharist as elsewhere it is only in Christ's glory that we make contact with his death. It is in Christ's glory that we sit down at the table of his sacrifice. He himself is present eating with us and nourishing us at one and the same time.

The Eucharist contains all that God in his love has done for us, it is the memorial of his wonderful works. Creation looks forward to the incarnation and redemption, and the redemption is the outpouring of the Spirit, the beginning of eternal life.

All this is in the Eucharist. Here we eat of the Risen Christ, God's own Son, from whose wounded side the Spirit comes to us giving us the adoption of sons. We go to the Body of Christ to receive the stream of living water, the Spirit and eternal life.

Each day we celebrate the Eucharist, the giving of thanks, taking our divine meal with gladness. Let us ask for the gifts of joy and gratitude that we may delight God in recognizing his marvellous love.

Reciprocal need

It would seem that for perfect mutual love two elements are necessary. In each of the lovers there must be a deep need for and a complete surrender to the other. Is this not so in human love? And our heart tells us that these two things must be found in the love between God and the soul.

Is there need in God? We are told God has no need of us, that he seeks only our good, that we cannot in any way enrich him. Surely these considerations, intended to demonstrate God's generous love, leave us a little cold? What lover likes to be told that the other feels no desire for love to be returned? Is this a true picture of God?

Let us turn to the Holy Scriptures. The Old Testament rings with the hurt of God, his grief at human ingratitude and disloyalty. He likens himself to a betrayed father, a deserted husband. And in the New Testament Jesus clearly expresses his need of affection, his yearning for love. 'Do you love me?' is his question to Peter. 'With desire I have desired,' he says at the Last Supper.

This desire finds its ultimate expression in the dying Christ: 'I thirst.' Thirst is a need of man which, if left unsatisfied, causes death. Such is God's need of me. It is his revelation: without your love I die. Knowledge which surpasses knowledge indeed!

A heart of mercy

God is the author of all tender-heartedness and goodness.

Misericors — a heart always inclined to another in compassion, a pitiful heart. A heart that is always good — that is, wishing good to another. Wherever we meet these qualities, there, we can be sure, is God.

We have to be perfect as our Father is perfect, and especially as he is perfect in these qualities.

Let me look at my heart. Is it unfailingly tender towards others? Unfailingly bent on their good? Or do I see that there is a lot of hardness there?

Am I perhaps kind to some but not to others? Kind at some times but not always? Not when I am upset, put out, hurt. . . Do I wish well to others only when their good doesn't conflict with what I think is mine?

God is the fount of tender-heartedness and goodness. Ask him for the grace to drink deeply of this fountain. Want these Godlike qualities with all your heart. Seize the opportunities each day offers to exercise them, no matter how much it costs pride and self-interest.

Chalice of salvation

Union with Jesus consists not in sitting in glory but in sharing his cup of shame, opprobrium, dishonour and powerlessness. These are the things in his mind when he offers us his cup, not the physical sufferings of his Passion.

How can we share this cup in our daily life?

By renouncing all power and every desire for it, every manoeuvre to obtain what we want, to prevail over others; by taking an attitude of unimportance and subjection to the community; by sacrificing the image we have of ourselves and which we sensitively want upheld in our own eyes and that of others; renouncing all desire for status and importance.

The cup Jesus wants to share with us is that of selfless love which is its own reward – he offers no other.

We think we know what the chalice contains and express our eagerness to drink it. When it comes to the point of drinking the above bitter ingredients, we turn away with loathing.

Our need of healing

An awareness of our sinfulness is part of holiness; you simply cannot have holiness without it for it is the inevitable effect of God's closeness. This is why true sorrow for sin is never morbid, depressed, for it carries within it the certainty of forgiveness.

The keenest sense of our guilt is thus bound up with the unfailing certainty of pardon; and the deepest contrition excludes all discouragement by renewing childlike trust. We should want compunction like this with all our hearts.

Scripture assures us that Jesus comes to heal our blindness, and blindness in regard to sin is our chief blindness. To a great extent, perhaps wholly, we choose how much we see. We cannot have God unless we are prepared to see ourselves, our lives, our past and present as they are, and half-consciously we know this revelation would be terrible. Therefore we make a choice not to see, or not to see very much.

Come and enlighten us, Sun of Holiness. Show us our sloth, our pride, our shirking of the demands of life, our evasions. Reveal to us our sinfulness in the light of your mercy, and then we shall be healed and know perfect joy.

Reconciliation

The particular aspect of our Lord's coming to us as a healer of our sinfulness is 'held' for us in a sacrament, a special 'moment'. As always with a sacrament there is a wedding of the human and the divine. Our part is to take our act of sorrow, paltry and inadequate as it is, to that heart which alone has gauged sin, taken its full weight.

Our poor sorrow is taken up, transformed into, the perfect reparation of Jesus.

When we run to our Father's arms in this sacrament we take the whole sinful but dearly-loved world with us. We hear the certain assurance: 'I forgive.' All our wrongs by him are righted. The Church is built up again, her broken walls restored in full.

Many of us, I think, were we to analyse our attitude to confession, would find our lack of zeal regarding it due to the sheer poverty of the rite. We are aware of the utter paltriness of our confession and sorrow. But that is just the point. It is Jesus' atoning love, his sorrow, that are going to matter.

True adoration

The patience of Jesus was the expression of his humble, adoring love. So it must be with us.

Humility does not consist in feeling wretched, miserable and so forth; one can feel all these things and not be humble at all. Humility means putting oneself aside, not considering self, thinking of others. It means seeing always the good and refusing to criticize.

Criticism of others always springs from wounded self-love, jealousy or some similar selfishness. Humility means making light of our own wounds and hurt feelings. This is true humility. In this way we offer God adoring love. It is a continual communion with the heart of Jesus.

In the light that falls on our souls from the eyes of the humbled Saviour we see ourselves: 'Human pride must be abased.'

More difficult to accept than humiliations from without are humiliations from within – the consciousness of our proneness to evil, forces we cannot control, inability to think of God and holy things... But prone in the mud we are one with Jesus.

This is the supreme moment. Now our adoration must rise up pure, intense, sweet, one with the adoration of Christ.

Abandonment

Let us realize that it is when self is prostrate, abased, that God is glorified. It is not that our misery of itself glorifies God, far from it! What glorifies him is that act of the will which, denying self, leaping up from the ashes of self, attains to him, singing with joy, 'Holy, holy, holy. You alone are the Lord.' Is there any act so utterly selfless as this? So pleasing to God?

Let us not think little of the times which may come to us when God touches our spirit and jubilantly our heart and flesh exult in the living God. Precious grace! But let us also appreciate at its full value if we can the opportunity more frequently given of being united to the Heart of Jesus in his prostration, 'a worm and no man', humbled, obedient unto death.

To live in this state of loving abandonment, accepting with patient love all that God permits to befall us, the state in which he permits us to be in, is to adore him in spirit and in truth.

Growing in intimacy

The consecrated woman consents to become a
'poor one' who, having abandoned all self-
reliance, expects everything from God; the 'poor
one' who, Scripture tells us, becomes the object of
God's special regard and self-giving love poured
out on her and the world she holds within her
heart.

Thus she perceives the other truth, 'power is made
perfect in weakness'.

In herself she represents the Church, the 'wife of
the Lamb', dependent solely on her Lord and
ceaselessly crying unto him. She longs to become
capable of pure love, 'one instance of which is
more precious in the eyes of God and the soul and
more profitable for the Church than all other good
works together'.

Truly blessed is she as she grows in intimacy with
the Lord. In this union lies her fulfilment as a
woman-person and her fruitfulness in the Church.

Humility is truth

Almost always God's greatest gifts are wrapped up in the sacking of painful self-knowledge. When we 'got on well' in prayer, when there was satisfaction in the Mass and sacraments, when we could talk inspiringly of spiritual things and others showed respect for our wisdom, we had no idea of the true state of affairs.

Humility is the acceptance of the truth about ourselves, not an effort to work up humble sentiments in spite of our obvious excellence! It is seeing and accepting the truth that we are not noble, good and spiritual.

This acceptance of lowliness means more to God than all our good works and fine intentions. What seems like loss and deprivation of blessings proves the very opposite.

God gives himself not in what exalts our ego, flatters our pride and self-conceit, but in what humbles us.

When God, All-Love, love that in its human expression sheds its last drop of blood for us, draws close . . . the ego is then shown up for what it is in all its distortion and ugliness.

God is our only joy

We have an instinctual drive towards seeking a sense of well-being in whatever way we conceive of it. Unchecked by reason it is likely to lead us to immediate satisfactions of one kind or another.

Hope is a similar drive which puts us in motion towards the attainment of our desired objective; we feel it is there to be had, that we have a right to it.

When our well-being is threatened we are afraid; we dread feeling 'unwell', unhappy, insecure, miserable, unattractive, downcast. . . We fear all that is inimical to what we conceive of as our happiness. When we lack the sense of well-being, we grieve.

But our true happiness lies in God and all our energy must be poured into surrendering to his will, not dissipated on things which eventually pall.

We must learn to make God our only joy and satisfaction, fearing only to miss him, to disappoint him; sad only for his grief.

This will not come easily, it must be struggled for.

Thy Kingdom come

When we pray 'Thy Kingdom come', we are inviting God to come and do in us all he wants to do. We are affirming that we want him to be our God and Father, to love us into fullness of life. We are praying that his great plan of love for creation be accomplished. Nothing else can satisfy the human heart he has made for himself.

We are utterly confident that God wants to give us his Kingdom and that he will leave no stone unturned to do so. There is therefore no need for strain or anxiety. There is no mysterious art to be mastered, it is all there before us at each moment.

What God asks of us we can always accomplish. There is nothing to be afraid of. It is not a chancy thing that might not come off.

Be happy to feel that you cannot control your life, that there is so much in you that you seem unable to cope with. Trust yourself to him, take each moment as it comes, for each moment holds him. Let him have the say, let him take charge, even though you are left feeling no one is in charge.

Dispossession of self is the reverse side of God-possession.

Sheep and goats

In the parable of the sheep and the goats Jesus makes it devastatingly clear that in the end it is only love of neighbour that counts — nothing else.

We shall not be examined on prayer, poverty, obedience or any of the other virtues; not because they are inessential but because they are real only in so far as we are wholly concerned with our neighbour.

You cannot pray, obey, or be truly poor, says our Lord, unless you are wholly taken up with your brother's needs.

No human heart is capable of such devotion, but Jesus asks it because what is impossible to man is possible to God. He has identified himself with us completely — 'you did it, did it not . . . to me' — so that he may be our life.

What he asks we can therefore fulfil if we really want to, if we pray from our hearts, if we really take the trouble to do all we can do.

Drawn into mystery

It was the love of the Father that pressed Jesus to die for love of us; his heart was beating with the Father's love. This is what we must long for, this selfless love of Jesus. Jesus crucified is the dark night into which we must enter so as to be one with God. We must allow ourselves to be drawn into mystery.

So the way to God is not by acquisition, not by building ourselves up, not by understanding but by letting go.

God himself will illumine our blindness, and this obscure knowledge is called mystical theology, the secret wisdom of God. We must renounce all clear perceptions of him and rest on faith alone.

Faith alone unites us to God; it is that journey of transcendence which leaves self so as to attain to God.

We have seen in Jesus the form it takes in this mortal life.

Gift of the Father

His own Son is the Father's gift to us, and we must creep into that Son's welcoming heart, content to shelter in his holiness, his goodness, his wisdom.

We have no holiness, goodness or wisdom of our own. So to be made consciously aware that we are spiritually inadequate, faulty, wretched – that we fail and sin – is a precious grace.

Pride would make us angry with ourselves or discouraged. Or on the other hand it might come into play further back and not allow us to become aware of our failings. It would provide us with the knack of sweeping them under the carpet so we did not have to face them.

Christian humility faces up to all this without anger or discouragement. It calls to mind that there was One who did the Father's will always; who offers the Father perfect love and worship. And this One is the Father's gift to us.

From the shelter of the Son's heart we go on trying, with him, to do always what pleases the Father; but at the same time never wanting to feel we are becoming holy and good, without spot or wrinkle.

Never are we more truly in Christ Jesus than when, deeply conscious of our sinfulness, we peacefully rest in the heart of the Redeemer – the Risen One.

Abba – Father

We belong to our holy Father, a hidden God, but in that hiddenness totally present. How then can we fritter away our lives as though they were unimportant? To be Father is to be life-giver, and God's deepest desire for us is fullness of life.

We must want this too. We must want to live each moment of our lives, really live, not just undergo. This means hoarding jealously the opportunities for growth – they come, are offered, they pass and never come again. They can be exploited or lost forever . . . unique opportunities of expressing our love and gratitude to him who loves us . . . of blind trust in him whom at present we cannot see or enjoy. Alas, that we value our lives so little and waste numerous occasions.

Jesus shows us what it is to hallow God's name. Not a moment of his precious life was frittered away, no occasion was lost, be it one of joy or sorrow.

It was in the same situation as we are, a situation of inherited weakness, trouble and temptation, that Jesus hallowed the name of his Father, flashing back to him, as in an untarnished mirror, his own self-giving.

In his deepest anguish he still murmured the tender name of 'Abba'. His lips uttered it but his *whole* being was ratifying 'You are my Abba, my holy Abba'.

Pure love

We must allow God to bring us to the fulfilment he has made us for, by a way that is infallible because it is his way for us. We must be brought to dispossession, emptiness, formlessness ... A dreadful prospect? Does not this spell death to a human being? Paradoxically, no, it is the other side of the plenitude of life.

The detached heart has a far greater joy and comfort in created realities, for to treat them possessively is to lose all joy in them.

The unselfish heart alone knows the joy of pure love for others. The more another is loved the more God is loved. Nothing is evil to the pure.

Generosity of heart, overflowing goodness, courage to face life and its demands, these are the fruits of true asceticism.

The pure of heart enjoy a hundredfold even in this life, finding joy in all that is, human or divine. Creation is restored to its true form and becomes the unsullied mirror of the face of God.

The surrendered Lord

The Father alone mattered to Jesus. He did not matter to himself at all. He left it to the Father to care for him; his whole substance was expended on him.

Jesus was so given, so surrendered, so emptied out, that he was like a hollow shell in which the roar of the ocean could be heard. He was an emptiness in which the Father could fully express his own self-giving being.

We have to be living embodiments of Jesus as he is of the Father. And this, says Jesus, is joy: 'My joy which you must share'.

It is Jesus who reveals what it means to be human. He is the light on the otherwise incomprehensible mystery of man.

Now that he is the Risen Lord, he knows whence he comes. He knows with the fullness of knowledge, in the full light of day and face to face, the Father from whom he draws his being, his meaning, his completion. He has reached his term, the goal of his developing, striving being – the Father.

Love of neighbour

When we hear those great, solemn, beautiful words intoned – 'Listen, Israel . . . You must love the Lord your God with all your heart and all your soul and all your strength' – we can feel deeply moved. They resound in our soul as the very meaning of life.

But what are we actually doing to live out this totality of love which constitutes the very existence of Jesus himself?

The love of God is impossible to evaluate. Love of neighbour is the only guide to its depths.

It is only in loving our neighbour that we can be set on loving God all the time and everywhere. There is no meaning to our human existence but this.

The more earnestly we want to surrender to God, the more determinedly we must work to love our neighbour.

Faith, not feeling

A Christian must live by faith, not feeling. My feeling is that I am of little consequence, inferior to others, not a nice sort of person; so I long to be important, someone of real worth, loved and considered precious. I tend therefore to be unhappy, rather envious of others. I am on the defensive, for I have to guard this little self which is always threatened. How then can I be wholly concerned with others? I can't let myself go, can't give, can't love.

But faith tells me that God loves me, that I am infinitely precious to him. I am made in his image, divine blood flows in my veins transfiguring me with beauty. I am fed on divine food, continually embraced by the Father. Oh yes, I recognize my frailty, but I know I am redeemed and that at every moment my frailty is supported, my sin cleansed, the radiance of divine love is my atmosphere.

Thus I learn to delight in myself, that I am I and no one else. I despise nothing in myself except the desire to stand on self. I thank God for what he has done in the unique situation which is my life. Even my sins and failures, the black shadows, are seen in the context of love, perhaps fulfilling the same role as pieces of black lead in a stained-glass window, making the colour even more glorious.

Perfect trust

Sometimes we can feel as if life is too hard, or just too uninteresting and drab. It can seem that the obstacles within ourselves are mountainous and insuperable. Jesus' own unwavering faith must be ours. Everything is possible to him who believes, was his humble boast.

When everything seemed to be going wrong for him, when the 'no' of human hearts had congealed into hard rock which threatened to grind him down, he was certain that the Father could and would remove the hard mass and drown it forever. He died in hope, not in hopes realized.

The picture of him asleep in a violent storm when others were frantic and angered by his seeming indifference reveals his inmost heart in its perfect trust.

If we would be his friends we must live like that. A friend of Jesus dares all and never says such and such is too hard. If God asks something, then it is possible of accomplishment. His friends evade nothing, be it trying situations, uncongenial people, difficult duties. They take each day as it comes with its pleasures and joys, its disagreeable things and pains. They shoulder their cross and go with Jesus.

The significance of the cross is not suffering but obedience — doing the Father's will regardless of whether it is easy or hard.

Let go and let God

We can fall into apathy, discouragement, and fail to correspond with God, continually bemoaning our state, whipping ourselves, indulging in self-pity, which is a covert way of getting at God. I dare not blame him so I blame myself and let off my resentment in that way.

I have to let go my poor aching self, drop myself, move out into the darkness to the certainty of God's love for me, of his goodness and fidelity. I know God loves me and will never reject me; he embraces sinners. What do my feelings matter? I will be at rest and refuse to lose heart. I will go on lifting my heart to him, knocking at the door, seeking, all the while knowing that he is with me and loves me.

All my feelings may scream against this but I do not trust anything in myself, only in God. I trust, not because I am good and therefore pleasing to him but because he is good and makes me pleasing to him by giving himself to me.

Now is the time to carry into reality the words of trust I have uttered, words of praise of God's goodness. Now is the time to show God I mean them.

The Dark Night and human experience

It would be wrong to assume that what John of the Cross speaks of as 'Dark Night' has nothing in common with ordinary, non-religious human experience. The image is not alien.

How many pages of literature, how many paintings and songs, have as their theme a dark night when what once had meaning now has none — when life's light has been extinguished, the heart bruised, the mind bewildered.

Bereavement, disappointment, failure, old age and, on the wider scene, the threat of atomic destruction; these and countless other common experiences engulf us in night.

All of them confront us with our finitude, raise fundamental questions on human existence and contain a challenge to accept our human vocation, whether we know the shape of that vocation or not.

Every human being is for God and an openness for God. It is not only around us who know his name but around every single person that the sun is shining, seeking an entrance. He uses every occasion to illumine us and his illumination is most often perceived as darkness.

Open to everything

Science, materialism, atheism do not banish God; they clear the atmosphere for true faith.

We can no longer confine God within the sacral and treat with him there. We must see him in all that is or not at all.

If we are weak in faith we may find his seeming absence unendurable, the effort to seek him in the world with all its attendant risks unbearable, and so we retreat into a ghetto, building up for ourselves a little world of spiritual make-believe which is safe, comfortable, unchallenged.

This is a powerful allure for some. It seems that *this* is the sphere of the holy where God is, whereas secularity is unholy and must be shunned.

If we would go forward, if we would surrender to God, we must keep our doors wide open. We must trustingly deal with the world, love it, enjoy it.

If we cling to our pietistic inwardness with its comfortable illusions of love for God and intimacy with him we shall never find him fully . . . preferring our sense of security to facing the living God.

Only his will matters

Under cover of spirituality we can be terribly self-willed, pursuing the path we have chosen for ourselves, manipulating those with authority over us or to whom we have given a measure of authority, so that they sanction our wishes and provide the spiritual security of 'God's will'.

He may be calling us to toil in his vineyard, bearing the burden and heat of the day, while we insist that we are called to a more austere form of life, a life of 'deeper prayer'.

On the other hand, it may be his will for us to live the contemplative life and we evade the renunciations and responsibilities of this vocation, encouraging a clientele which flatters our pride and provides continual diversion.

Let us remind ourselves over and over again that holiness has to do with very ordinary things: truthfulness, kindness, gentleness, contentment with our lot, consideration for others, honesty and courage in the face of life, reliability, dutifulness.

Intent, as we think, on the higher reaches of spirituality, we can overlook the warp and woof of holiness.

Forgiveness

Jesus says that our Father will not forgive us unless we forgive each other from our hearts. It is not that he will not but that he cannot. An unforgiving heart is closed to receiving the rivers of Christ's redemptive love.

'Do not judge', because you simply cannot know the truth about someone else's motives. Only God can know the mysterious depth of the human heart. When we judge, what we are actually saying is that if *I* did or said so and so it would be because I was angry, jealous, etc. But we presume to add, *they* do this therefore *they* are angry, jealous, etc. They mean to hurt me.

By making a habit based on Jesus' teaching (but also on common sense and experience) of reflecting that we simply *cannot* know another's motives, we are forced into blind trust in our neighbours, and that is wonderful.

I am convinced that this resolution, consistently practised, produces a pure, constant, tender love for all.

What greater blessing could we wish for, and what better way to ensure our openness to Jesus so that he can use us as channels of his love.

Dives and Lazarus

In the parable of Dives and Lazarus, Dives closed his heart to God. It was not because he was rich that he failed but because he closed his heart to God before him in the other person.

The other person did not matter to him. He didn't beat him or drive him off; he just ignored him because he was wrapped up in himself.

Our Lazarus need not be a pauper. Lazarus is merely the person who is not myself – the other – with their own individuality and their own outlook and needs.

We need each other. None of us is truly rich and sooner or later each of us suffers from ignoring the other. It is our mutual privilege to give to one another.

I must pray for the humility to realize that I need – and thus humbly hold out my little cup for the water of another whom, in my deepest heart, I have thought little of.

Authority is service

In Jesus' eyes, human authority has a very lowly place: limited, without grandeur or fine titles, with no advantages whatever for the ones holding authority but only for those at whose service they are.

If we hold any sort of authority, either as an individual or as a group, we must avoid laying unnecessary burdens on those concerned. God never does this. His disciples must recognize this and refuse to offer cult or incense to any human authority.

Jesus wants every one of his disciples to be wholly detached from desire for human recognition, praise, status, popularity. If we want these things (as opposed to merely liking them) then we cut ourselves off from Jesus who wanted nothing but the Father's glory.

Only our grasp that we have a Father in heaven and a supreme Master in Jesus can enable us to live in our simple dignity without craving for false esteem.

Self-emptying love

Because Jesus is emptied out the Father is free to give himself as he wants to, totally and without measure. Thus everything the Father is, Jesus is; everything the Father does, Jesus does.

Jesus' self-emptying love attained its completion on the cross, 'It is consummated', and was itself the human expression of the Father's love.

We learn here that the very essence of the Father is to be self-giving love, a love that keeps nothing back, that is totally ecstatic. We see what we could never have dreamed of, omnipotence that operates only in weakness and self-sacrifice.

Oh where is the God of glory our pride so desires! No wonder that if we would reach our fulfilment in a mystery of love such as this we must walk in a way we know not, must allow ourselves to die to our own selfish, limited earthly ideas and permit ourselves to be led unknowing into the darkness which is in reality the radiant light of a love too pure for our self-reflecting eyes.

Union and communion

The Eucharist is the most sacred act of the day;
the memorial of the Lord's death
and resurrection,
a sacrament of love,
a sign of unity,
a banquet
where joyfully we partake
of the living Bread
come down from heaven,
and drink the chalice
of his Blood.

The mind is filled with grace
and a pledge of future glory
is given to us.

With all our heart we unite ourselves to Jesus
in his surrender to the Father.

Give us this day our daily bread —
the bread of your Will,
the bread of your Body.

A *living response*

The Church's children bring the bread and wine, fruit of the earth and work of human hands, symbols of the offering of ourselves.

These are laid upon the altar with our poor lives, each day, each hour ... filled with little actions, fears, longings, sufferings – all that goes to make up a human span – but in sacrifice. We want these poor earthly things to be an expression of perfect love for the Father.

We give you, Lord, all that we have and are under the veil of bread and wine. In themselves as of themselves they are ineffective, they can never carry us to the Father. Make them into your own offering, your own flight of love which does get there. Transform us into your immolated self.

In Holy Communion we receive back the humble offerings we first presented, not as themselves but as sacrament of union, of transformation. We eat God and are transformed thereby.

Not that we become something marvellous, but so that we become nothing but a living response, an act of obedience, a pure burnt-offering.

Thus we too will shine with the light of Godhead – but he alone will see it.

Realizing our potential

To say God is within us is to say we are transcendent, for God, our being subsisting in him and for him. He is our centre, our term, our completion.

Mystical contemplation is a divine impetus, vivifying, energizing, bringing into realization what is already there, as at the call of spring the seed begins to germinate. This is scriptural teaching. We must be born again of the Spirit. Without the Spirit we remain flesh which cannot know God.

The evolution of the butterfly is a marvellous image of what is meant here. The caterpillar must be 'born again'; it must receive an impetus to enable it to be transformed into a butterfly, but it has within it, in its caterpillar state, all the potential for this. Nothing new is added, what is there is fully developed.

So it is with us. God is our Beloved in truth now, but will be so even more truly when we can call him that after long and generous efforts and correspondence with his action. Then we are no longer our own but his.

From darkness to light

God is darkness in this life but a blessed darkness, a darkness our deepest self wants. Anything less than the All which, being no-thing, total mystery, must be darkness to us, would never satisfy us. We cannot have it both ways – a God made to our own measure, even our finest measure, whom we can grasp with our minds, and at the same time perfect human fulfilment.

Loyally we must accept him in darkness, refuse to identify him with any means to him no matter how sublime and spiritual these may seem. We must not try to drag him out of his secrecy, but desire with intense desire to be taken into it.

Thus everything, natural goods, moral goods, spiritual perceptions, illuminations, gifts of no matter how high and rare a kind, the most lofty communications that can be conceived – all these are things, creatures, means, and far, far removed from him. Our tendency is always to turn them into idols, substitute them for the impenetrable mystery.

Faith is therefore a constant stripping of what we understand to be God in order that God may be what he is in his own reality: it is a flight from where we are to where he is.

Walking with God

'Enoch walked with God and was not, for God took him.'

Here is the essence of the human vocation – to allow God to be close every day, every hour. It is to live one's life nakedly exposed to him, walking with him, allowing his dangerous nearness ('our God is a consuming fire').

We are told by the same writer of Genesis that this is what God intends for all; but men reject it, escape from God, struggle to hide their nakedness, their poverty, because they cannot bear to live with nothing of themselves, completely surrendered to a love which purifies and transforms.

Carmel is ideally Eden restored, but let us not romanticize. The essence of Eden is God's closeness and the exposure of human nakedness in perfect trust, growing intimacy.

Of a Carmelite it should be said not that she was an efficient prioress or bursar, she was so charming and clever, she was such a hard worker, but . . . she walked with God. She allowed his fire to burn away her ego, she lived in nakedness, she simply disappeared and there was only Jesus left. She 'died' and therefore could never see death, physical death had completely changed its nature for her.

Life in the light

The Bride lives in light, surrounded by it, penetrated by it from every angle. Because it is unimpeded, naked, full, circumambient, it is essentially formless, like an atmosphere.

For most of us light can get at us here and there, now from this angle, now from that, and more persistently as we progress. But for the Bride the inflow of light is total.

She always sees God, always loves him in the multiple concrete demands of every day. She is never 'not there', never unprepared.

Hers is real, solid virtue; a habit that is the effect of great, constant love. 'I do always the things that please him.' Hers is inviolable strength, not as from herself, for she remains poor and weak, as well she knows, but from the God who possesses her and communicates to her his own strength. She lives by his life, his virtue, his wisdom, his love; hence her utter security.

She has chosen to abandon all for his sake . . . So now God assumes full care of her, holds her in his arms, feeds her with all good things and takes her into his deepest secrets.

Sources and index

The following abbreviations have been used for the Source references in the index. Figures in bold type refer to the pages of Readings in this book.

GMP: *Guidelines to Mystical Prayer** (Sheed and Ward 1976)
TBJ: *To Believe in Jesus** (Sheed and Ward 1978)
ICE: *Interior Castle Explored** (Sheed and Ward 1981)
LL: *Living Love* (DLT 1985)
OF: *Our Father* (DLT 1986)
AL: *Ascent to Love* (DLT 1986)
GE: *Garden Enclosed* (printed privately)
UC: Unpublished Conferences

*For copyright reasons it has only been possible to take one extract from each of these books. These three extracts are used by permission of Sheed and Ward Ltd.

33 UC	**47** *GMP* 36
34 *GE* 13	**48** *AL* 57
35 *AL* 58	**49** *AL* 101
36 *AL* 32	**50** *ICE* 19
37 *OF* 36	**51** *OF* 55
38 *LL* 41	**52** *LL* 52
39 *AL* 83	**53** *LL* 44
40 *LL* 22	**54** *AL* 82
41 *OF* 33	**55** *GE* 18
42 *AL* 47	**56** *OF* 48
43 *OF* 40	**57** *AL* 19
44 *LL* 48	**58** *AL* 73
45 UC	**59** UC
46 *OF* 21	**60** *AL* 115